TIMELINES ▶ The Iraq War

Paul Mason

ARCTURUS

This edition first published in 2010 by Arcturus Publishing
Distributed by Black Rabbit Books
P.O. Box 3263
Mankato
Minnesota MN 56002

Copyright © 2010 Arcturus Publishing Limited

Printed in China

Library of Congress Cataloging-in-Publication Data

Mason, Paul.
 The Iraq War / Paul Mason.
    p. cm. -- (Timelines)
 Summary: "Discusses events in Iraq that lead up to the current war in Iraq,
beginning with the end of the Persian Gulf War and continuing through the
planned withdrawal for all coalition forces from the country"--Provided by
publisher.
 Includes bibliographical references and index.
 ISBN 978-1-84837-639-7 (library bound)
 1. Iraq War, 2003---Juvenile literature. 2. Iraq--Politics and government--2003---
Juvenile literature. I. Title.
 DS79.763.M38 2011
 956.7044'3--dc22
                        2009051266

The right of Paul Mason to be identified as the author of this work has been asserted by him in accordance
with the Copyright, Designs and Patents Act 1988.

Series concept: Alex Woolf
Editor and picture researcher: Nicola Barber
Consultant: James Vaughan
Designer: Ariadne Ward
Illustrator: Stefan Chabluk

Picture credits:
Corbis: cover (Jerome Sessini), 4 (Peter Turnley), 5 (Peter Turnley), 6 (Ed Kashi), 8 (Rick Maiman/Sygma),
9 (Samara Boustani/Sygma), 10 (Leonhard Foeger/Reuters), 11 (Faleh Kheiber/Reuters), 12 (Bob E.
Daemmrich/Sygma), 13 (Faleh Kheiber/Reuters), 14 (Najlah Feanny), 15 (Rune Hellestad), 16 (Olivier
Coret), 17 (Oleg Popov/Reuters), 19 (Jerome Sessini), 20 (Larry Downing/Reuters), 21 (Thorne Anderson),
22 (Michael Appleton), 23 (Ali Jasim/Reuters), 25 (handout/Reuters), 26 (Scott Nelson/epa), 27 (Ali
Abbas/epa), 29 (Paul Buck/epa), 30 (Ceerwan Aziz/Reuters), 31 (Chris Helgren/Reuters), 32 (Johancharles
Van Boers/US Army/ZUMA), 33 (Namir Noor-Eldeen/Reuters), 34 (Zohra Bensemra/Reuters), 35 (Ali
Haider/Pool/Reuters), 37 (Wael Al-Samarraie/epa), 38 (Steven Clevenger), 39 (Ali Abbas/epa), 40 (epa),
41 (Larry Downing/Reuters), 43 (Azad Lashkari/Reuters), 44 (Nawras al-Ta'El/epa).
Rex Features: 18, 24 (Sipa Press), 28 (Sabah Arar), 36, 42 (Sipa Press), 45.
Cover picture: A US soldier covers a statue of Saddam Hussein with a US flag after the fall of Baghdad, 2003.

Every attempt has been made to clear copyright. Should there be any inadvertent omission, please apply to
the publisher for rectification.

ISBN: 978-1-84837-639-7
SL001323US
Supplier 03, Date 0210

Contents

Defeat and Humiliation

Bombed vehicles litter the "highway of death" in March 1991. Many Iraqi soldiers died on this road, which leads from Kuwait to Iraq, as they tried to retreat.

On March 3, 1991, the world's eyes were fixed on Safwan Airfield—a small, dusty air base north of the Iraq-Kuwait border. But what was it about this tiny place that was so important? The answer is that it was where Iraq's attempt to occupy its southern neighbor, Kuwait, finally failed. Here, Iraq's army surrendered to US general "Storming" Norman Schwarzkopf.

INVADING KUWAIT

Iraqi forces invaded Kuwait on August 2, 1990, and they quickly took control of the whole country. For many years Iraq had been claiming that Kuwait was really part of its territory. This claim was based on the fact that before either country existed, Kuwait had once been part of the province of Basra, which was now part of Iraq. Also,

Iraq owed Kuwait over $8 billion it had borrowed during an earlier war, against Iran, between 1980 and 1988. Taking over Kuwait, and gaining control of Kuwait's valuable oil reserves, meant these debts would disappear.

INTERNATIONAL REACTION

Four days after Iraq's invasion began, the United Nations (UN) imposed sanctions on Iraq and demanded that Iraqi forces leave Kuwait. The UN began to gather together an international

Vital oil supplies

"I will not allow this little dictator to control 25 percent of the world's oil." President George H. W. Bush speaking about Saddam Hussein after Iraq's invasion of Kuwait.

TIMELINE	**IRAQ AND KUWAIT, 1930s–1991**
1930s	▶ King Ghazi of Iraq claims that Kuwait should be part of Iraq.
1961	▶ Iraqi leader General Qasim lays claims to Kuwait.
September 22, 1980	▶ Iraq invades Iran, starting a war that will last until August 20, 1988. By the end of the war, Iraq owes the countries that supported it an estimated $65–75 billion.
August 2, 1990	▶ Iraq invades Kuwait.
February 27, 1991	▶ The last Iraqi troops are driven from Kuwait.
March 3, 1991	▶ Iraq surrenders to UN coalition forces.

coalition—armed forces that would be able to drive the Iraqis from Kuwait. Iraq's leader, Saddam Hussein, refused to withdraw his army, so on January 16, 1991, the UN coalition attacked, starting the Persian Gulf War. By the end of February, Iraq's troops had been defeated. Kuwait had been freed, and Saddam no longer controlled roughly a quarter of the world's reserves of oil, a crucial resource.

AFTER THE DEFEAT

After defeating Iraq, the UN wanted to make sure that Saddam Hussein would not be able to threaten his neighbors again. In particular, the UN was worried about Iraq's attempts to manufacture weapons of mass destruction (WMDs). These are weapons such as nuclear bombs, chemical weapons, or biological weapons that can kill large numbers of people. The Iraqi army had already used chemical weapons during the war with Iran, as well as against its own people, as a way of keeping control of the country. Resolution 687, passed by the UN in April 1991, called on Iraq to surrender its WMDs and to destroy any facilities capable of making such weapons. Saddam was also forced to agree that UN officials, known as weapons inspectors, would be allowed to come into Iraq to monitor the ban.

CROSS-REFERENCE
KURDISH AND SHIA
REBELLIONS:
PAGES 6–7 ▶

As the Iraqis left Kuwait, they set the country's oil wells alight. Many of the wells burned for weeks.

Kurdish Safe Haven

On April 5, 1991, the UN Security Council called on Iraq to end its attacks on the Kurdish people who live in northern Iraq. (Kurds also live in other countries, including Turkey and Iran.) During the Persian Gulf War, the Kurds had taken the side of the UN coalition, and as the war drew to an end, they had rebelled against Saddam's rule. Many Kurds did not want to be part of Iraq and hoped that they would one day have their own country, Kurdistan.

KURDISH REBELLION

In March 1991, Saddam's forces put down a rebellion by the Kurds using artillery and bombing. The UN feared that Saddam Hussein would take a terrible revenge on the Kurds for opposing him. His forces had treated the Kurds brutally in the past. Between 1987 and 1989, Saddam's cousin Ali Hassan al-Majid had organized a series of attacks, known as the al-Anfal campaign, which caused the deaths of at least 120,000 Kurds. In one of the worst attacks, in the Kurdish town of Halabja, chemical weapons had been used to kill around 3,200 people. Thousands more died in the years after the attack from the effects of the poison gas.

PROTECTING THE KURDS

On March 3, 1991, General Schwarzkopf warned the Iraqi air force that any planes flying over Kurdish areas would be shot down. The United States, Britain, and Turkey then began to establish a "no-fly zone" in northern Iraq. Without air support, it was impossible for Saddam to attack the Kurds. For the next six years, the Iraqis largely respected the no-fly zone, and from January 1, 1997 it became known as Operation Northern Watch.

OPERATION SOUTHERN WATCH

On August 27, 1992, the United States, Britain, France, and Saudi Arabia set up Operation Southern

Kurdish men examine an Iraqi bomb that contains chemical weapons. Fortunately, the bomb did not explode when it landed in 1988.

THE KURDS, 1978–1997

1978–1979 ▶	The Iraqi army burns down 600 Kurdish villages and deports 200,000 Kurds to other parts of Iraq.
March 29, 1987 ▶	The start of the al-Anfal campaign by the Iraqi army against the Kurds, which ends on April 23, 1989.
March 16–17, 1988 ▶	Iraq attacks the Kurdish town of Halabja using poison gas.
March 1991 ▶	Uprisings against Saddam in Iraqi Kurdistan and Shia areas of the south are suppressed by the Iraqi government using artillery and helicopter bombers.
April 10, 1991 ▶	The United States orders Iraq to end all military activity in Iraqi Kurdistan.
January 1, 1997 ▶	Operation Northern Watch is established.

This map shows the limits of the northern and southern no-fly zones in Iraq. Iraqi planes in these areas risked being attacked by US or British fighter aircraft.

Watch. This was another no-fly zone, this time in southern Iraq. The aim was to protect Iraq's Shia Muslim population, which lived mainly in the south. Like the Kurds, the Shia had unsuccessfully rebelled against Saddam in 1991.

CONFLICT OVER THE NO-FLY ZONES

On December 16, 1998, US forces began a bombing campaign against Iraqi weapons factories called Operation Desert Fox. In response, Iraq announced it would no longer respect the no-fly zones.

CROSS-REFERENCE OPERATION DESERT FOX: PAGES 8–9

Iraq's peoples

Iraq is made up of three main groups of people:

- **Shia Muslims, living mainly in the southern part of the country. The Shia follow the same religion as most people in neighboring Iran.**
- **Sunni Muslims, who live mostly in a central strip of Iraq, including the capital city, Baghdad. Under Saddam, Sunnis dominated Iraq's government.**
- **Kurds, who live in northern Iraq (as well as other nearby countries).**

Weapons Inspection Clashes

OCTOBER 29, 1997

On October 29, 1997, Iraq announced that it would no longer allow American UN weapons inspectors into the country. Saddam Hussein considered the United States to be an enemy of Iraq because it had led the coalition that forced his army to leave Kuwait. He claimed that the UN Special Commission (UNSCOM) set up to inspect the ban on WMDs in Iraq was full of American spies.

A CAT-AND-MOUSE GAME

The dispute about US weapons inspectors was the start of a cat-and-mouse game between the United States and the UN on one side and Iraq on the other. Saddam would agree to allow inspections, then block the inspectors or only allow them limited access to weapons sites. Then, just as it seemed the UN might act, he would allow inspections again.

INSPECTIONS ON: After the October 1997 announcement, Russia suggested a compromise agreement, which Iraq at first accepted.
OFF: On January 13, 1998, Iraq stopped an inspection by a US-dominated team, and accused its leader, Scott Ritter, of spying.
ON: On February 23, 1998, UN secretary general Kofi Annan met

Saddam in Baghdad and announced a new deal on weapons inspections.
OFF: Then, on October 31, 1998, the Iraqi leadership said it would no longer cooperate with UNSCOM.
ON: On November 14, after it became clear that the international community was determined that weapons inspections should continue, Iraq said inspections could begin again. UNSCOM inspection teams returned to Iraq on November 17, 1998.
OFF: This time, it was the UN that canceled the inspections. On December 16, 1998, the UN ordered all its weapons inspectors to leave Iraq. The head of UNSCOM, Richard Butler, issued a report saying the Iraqis were refusing to cooperate, making the inspectors' jobs impossible.

A UN weapons inspector in Iraq tests a container to find out if it holds chemical or biological weapons.

TIMELINE

IRAQ AND WMDs, 1959–1991

August 17, 1959 ▶ The Soviet Union and Iraq sign an agreement to develop an Iraqi nuclear power station.

April 1975 ▶ Saddam Hussein visits Moscow and asks for nuclear help. The Soviet Union refuses.

1980s ▶ Companies from many countries sell Iraq material that can be used for WMDs.

November 1980 ▶ Iraq's first use of chemical weapons in the Iran-Iraq War.

June 7, 1981 ▶ Israel destroys Iraq's Osirak nuclear reactor in an air raid.

April 3, 1991 ▶ UN Security Council Resolution 687 forbids Iraq from having chemical, biological, or nuclear weapons.

OPERATION DESERT FOX

Hours after the UNSCOM teams left Iraq, Operation Desert Fox began. This was a series of air attacks by the United States and Britain on December 16 and 17, aimed at destroying suspected Iraqi weapons sites. Iraq retaliated by firing at patrolling US and British planes. As a result of Operation Desert Fox, most of Iraq's air defense missile sites were destroyed.

Protesters demonstrate in Baghdad against the UN's weapons inspections in Iraq. They are waving photos of President Saddam Hussein to show their support for him.

CROSS-REFERENCE
WEAPONS
INSPECTIONS:
PAGES 10–13

What the inspectors found

By the time they left Iraq in December 1998, the UNSCOM inspection teams had found and destroyed

- 48 long-range missiles
- 14 conventional missile warheads
- 30 chemical weapon warheads
- supplies for a "supergun" able to fire long distances
- almost 40,000 chemical munitions
- 628 tons of chemical weapons agents
- a biological weapons plant

The teams also discovered evidence of a program to develop nuclear weapons.

UNMOVIC

On December 17, 1999, the UN Security Council passed Resolution 1284. This created a new weapons inspection organization to replace UNSCOM. The new organization was called the UN Monitoring, Verification, and Inspection Commission, or UNMOVIC.

Breaking the deadlock

The creation of UNMOVIC was partly an attempt by the UN to end the cat-and-mouse game between the UN and Iraq over weapons inspections. By replacing the old organization with a new one, the UN was reinforcing the message that the weapons inspection teams were international, not American. From March 1, 2000, UNMOVIC was led by a Swede, Hans Blix.

Saddam tries to negotiate

When Iraq invaded Kuwait in 1990, the UN imposed trade restrictions, or sanctions, on Iraq. Until the sanctions began, Iraq had used income from the export of oil to buy goods such as food, clothing, medical supplies, and machinery from other countries. Under the UN sanctions, Iraq was banned from selling its oil. The sanctions, which continued after the end of the war, had a disastrous effect in Iraq, causing widespread shortages of food and other supplies. By 2000, Saddam was desperate for the UN's sanctions to be relaxed. He tried to use the issue of weapons inspections as a bargaining point by saying that he would allow UN inspections teams

into Iraq if the sanctions were eased. The UN—Britain and the United States in particular—began to suspect that these negotiations were a way of keeping the inspectors out so that Iraq could go on developing WMDs. On September 12, 2002, President George W. Bush warned Iraq that it could be attacked unless it complied with UN resolutions on disarmament and weapons inspections.

Pressure on Iraq increases

Pressure on Iraq over WMDs began to increase. Both Britain and the United States began to release information suggesting that Iraq was trying to develop new WMDs. On September 24, 2002, the British government produced a document

Hans Blix, the UN's chief weapons inspector for Iraq, speaks to the press in September 2002. Two weeks earlier, President Bush had warned Iraq that it would be attacked unless it went along with weapons inspections.

WEAPONS INSPECTION NEGOTIATIONS, 2002

July 5, 2002 ▶ Two days of UN-Iraq talks about weapons inspections end without agreement.

September 16, 2002 ▶ The Iraqi government offers to allow the return of weapons inspectors.

September 28, 2002 ▶ Iraq rejects a draft UN resolution with strict new rules for weapons inspections.

October 1, 2002 ▶ Hans Blix and Iraq agree to practical arrangements for the return of weapons inspectors. The United States says it wants a tough new UN Security Council agreement instead.

October 11, 2002 ▶ The US Senate authorizes President Bush to use force against Iraq.

October 25, 2002 ▶ The United States puts a new plan for disarming Iraq to the UN Security Council.

November 4, 2002 ▶ Saddam Hussein says Iraq will comply with a new UN plan as long as it does not serve as an excuse for US military action.

Members of an Iraqi family head for home in May 2001 with their monthly food ration. The food had probably reached Iraq through the UN's "oil for food" agreement, which allowed Iraq to sell oil as a way of paying for food and medicines.

claiming that
- Iraq was developing new WMDs and nuclear weapons
- Iraq had recently imported nuclear weapons uranium from Niger
- Iraq could have WMDs ready for use in 45 minutes

All these claims later turned out to be mistaken.

CROSS-REFERENCE
THE HUNT FOR WMDs:
PAGES 18–19

9/11

On September 11, 2001, al-Qaeda terrorists hijacked four passenger planes and used them to attack targets in the United States. Two planes hit the World Trade Center in New York City, destroying it. The third attacked the Pentagon, and the fourth crashed into the ground. In all, almost 3,000 people were killed. The attacks made the US government determined to root out Islamist terrorism around the world. The United States and its Western allies became even more concerned about Iraq's suspected WMD program. They feared that Iraq might ally itself with terrorists and supply them with WMDs.

Resolution 1441

President George W. Bush and British prime minister Tony Blair hold a joint press conference in 2002. The two leaders were close allies in the lead-up to the invasion of Iraq.

By late 2002, the United States and Britain had become convinced that Saddam Hussein would never deal honestly with the UN. They began to try to persuade other countries that action had to be taken. In response, on November 8, 2002 the UN Security Council passed a new resolution on Iraq's disarmament. Resolution 1441 warned Iraq that there would be "serious consequences" if it failed to follow the new rules on WMDs and weapons inspections.

USE OF FORCE

Resolution 1441 did *not* say that Iraq would be attacked unless it went along with the resolution's terms. President George W. Bush and British prime minister Tony Blair tried to persuade other countries that an attack might be needed, but they did not succeed. Led by President Jacques Chirac of France, the leaders of other countries, including Germany and Russia, felt that it should still be possible to persuade Saddam to agree to weapons inspections.

IRAQI ACCEPTANCE

On November 13, 2002, Iraq told the UN that it would agree to Resolution 1441. That same day, UN weapons inspectors arrived in Baghdad, ready to start work again. Under Resolution 1441, Iraq had to submit a report describing what had already been done to destroy its WMDs and weapons factories. It presented this report to the UN on December 7, and it seemed that Saddam was finally submitting to the UN. But then, on December 19, 2002, Hans Blix told the UN that he thought the report mostly contained information already released by Iraq five years previously, in 1997.

TIMELINE

MOVING TOWARD CONFLICT, 2002–2003

November 8, 2002 ▶ The UN Security Council unanimously passes Resolution 1441 on Iraq's disarmament, warning of "serious consequences" if Iraq does not stick to the rules.

November 13, 2002 ▶ Iraq's government accepts the UN resolution.

November 18, 2002 ▶ Hans Blix leads UN inspectors back to Baghdad to start their mission.

March 17, 2003 ▶ The weapons inspectors are withdrawn.

THE PATH TO WAR

By early 2003, the United States and its allies seemed determined to attack Iraq. This determination was strengthened on January 27, when the weapons inspectors reported that they were not getting full cooperation from the Iraqis. A coalition made up of the United States and a relatively small number of other countries began to build up forces in preparation for war. On March 17, 2003, Britain's ambassador to the UN said the diplomatic process on Iraq had ended. The arms inspectors were evacuated. President Bush gave Saddam Hussein and his sons 48 hours to leave Iraq— or face war.

CROSS-REFERENCE
ANTI-WAR PROTESTS: PAGES **14–15**
THE INVASION: PAGES **16–17**

Weapons inspectors, wearing hats in UN blue to identify themselves, arrive at Baghdad airport to leave Iraq in March 2003.

Lethal weapons?

"In Iraq [Saddam Hussein] is building and hiding weapons that could enable him to dominate the Middle East and intimidate the civilized world— and we will not allow it."
President George W. Bush, speaking in February 2003.

Protests Against War

In the United States, demonstrators took to the streets near the UN headquarters in New York City, despite a judge having earlier denied them permission to hold a march.

Around the world, many people felt unhappy about the way the US and British governments, in particular, were heading toward war against Iraq. On February 15, 2003, in cities around the world, many people took to the streets to protest against the coming war. Exactly how many people took part in the protests is not agreed, but the number was probably somewhere between 6 and 10 million people. It was the largest protest in human history.

THE PROTEST MOVEMENT

Protest against a possible conflict with Iraq had been increasing for several months. The protesters felt that the disagreements could be resolved through continued negotiations. Some suggested that the great prize of Iraq's huge oil reserves, rather than WMDs, was the real reason for the conflict. In January 2003, there were anti-war rallies in many cities around the world. There

is no definite agreement about how many people took part in the February 15, 2003 anti-war protests. The organizers usually make high estimates, and many people think the police make low ones. In total, the protests took place in over 60 countries:

• In Rome, Italy, 3 million people demonstrated.
• In London, UK, between 1 and 2 million people took part.
• In Barcelona, Spain, 1.3 million protested.
• In Australia's state capitals, 500,000 people took part.
• In San Francisco, there were 200,000 protesters and in New York City, 100,000.

REACTION TO THE PROTESTS

The governments of the United States and its allies did not change their plans as a result of the protests. They continued to prepare for war. Prime Minister John Howard of Australia seemed to sum up the leaders' attitude when he claimed: "I don't know that you can measure public opinion just by the

TIMELINE

ANTI-WAR PROTESTS, 2002–2003

September 12, 2002 ▸ A small crowd gathers outside the UN General Assembly as President George W. Bush speaks there.

September 27, 2002 ▸ Between 150,000 and 400,000 people attend a rally in London.

October 2002 ▸ Protests around the world, with hundreds of thousands of people joining demonstrations in many major cities.

November 9, 2002 ▸ Between half a million and a million people demonstrate in Florence, Italy.

January 18, 2003 ▸ Protests against war in towns and cities around the world.

February 15, 2003 ▸ Enormous worldwide protests against war.

number of people that turn up at demonstrations." And in the United States, surveys showed that most people supported war in Iraq: in March 2003, 72 percent of Americans thought the use of military force in Iraq was "the right decision".

ANTI-WAR PROTESTS CONTINUE

Anti-war protests continued even after the war had begun. Because the demonstrators had by then failed in their main aim—to persuade their governments to abandon the idea of war against Iraq—the size of the protests slowly decreased.

On February 15, 2003, the Reverend Jesse Jackson spoke to a huge crowd in London. On this same day, people in many of the world's cities demonstrated against a war in Iraq that was starting to seem inevitable.

**CROSS-REFERENCE
THE INVASION
AND THE FALL OF
BAGHDAD: PAGES
16–19**

Alternative views

"The inspectors say that [Iraqi] cooperation has improved and that they are in a position to pursue their work. This is what is essential. It's not up to you or me to say if the inspections are working. We refuse to follow a path that will lead automatically to war as long as the inspectors don't say to us, 'We can't go any further.'"
President Jacques Chirac of France, March 11, 2003.

"I'm not opposed to all wars. I'm opposed to dumb wars."
Senator (and later President) Barack Obama speaks at a small-scale anti-war protest in Chicago, October 2, 2003.

Invasion

On the second day of the war, March 21, 2003, the US campaign of heavy bombing—known as "shock and awe"—devastates parts of Baghdad.

On March 19, 2003, the ultimatum President Bush had given Saddam Hussein—that he and his sons must leave Iraq within 48 hours—ran out. The next day, the coalition's invasion of Iraq began. The US commanders named it "Operation Iraqi Freedom." They thought that a successful invasion would set the Iraqi people free from the rule of the cruel tyrant Saddam.

THE COALITION

The United States had wanted to involve as many countries as possible in the coalition. However, only five countries—Australia, Denmark, Poland, Spain and Britain—sent troops to help the United States in the invasion of Iraq. More than 30 other countries did later provide support for the coalition. But many of the world's leaders did not feel that the weapons inspections teams had been given a chance to finish their job and saw no reason to support the war. Some people also felt that WMDs were not the real reason for the war. Their view was that President Bush was more interested in gaining control over Iraq's large oil reserves.

IRAQI FORCES

Estimates of the size of the Iraqi force facing the coalition vary. Many records have been lost or destroyed, and today no one is absolutely certain how many people were in the Iraqi military and paramilitary. However, the International Institute for Strategic Studies estimated that Iraqi military forces numbered 538,000. On top of this, there were 44,000 Fedayeen Saddam (paramilitary forces loyal to the government of Saddam Hussein) and 80,000 Republican Guards. But Saddam's forces lacked the latest weapons, and many of their planes and air defense sites had been destroyed in bombing attacks before the invasion began.

| TIMELINE | LEAD-UP TO THE INVASION, 2002 |

LEAD-UP TO THE INVASION, 2002

July 2002 ▶ Members of the Special Activities Division of the CIA are parachuted into Iraq to prepare for a possible invasion.

September 5, 2002 ▶ Air attacks on Iraqi targets are launched from no-fly zones. They destroy the main air defense site in western Iraq.

September 2002 onwards ▶ The United States and Britain increase bombing raids against Iraqi ground targets.

THE INVASION

On March 20, US missiles began to hit targets in Baghdad. In the following days, coalition ground troops entered Iraq from the south. Paratroopers landed in northern Iraq, opening a second front. At first, the coalition met pockets of stiff resistance. The Iraqi army and irregular forces splintered, then gathered around strategic points. One of these was the port of Umm Qasr, where the Iraqis resisted the invading forces for a week. Eventually, however, the coalition's superior firepower began to tell, and its forces began to make rapid progress toward Baghdad.

CROSS-REFERENCE
ANTI-WAR PROTESTS: PAGES 14–15

Iraqi soldiers, who have dressed in civilian clothes to try to avoid capture, are escorted by US soldiers in March 2003.

Troop numbers—Operation Iraqi Freedom

Troops from six countries were sent to take part in the invasion of Iraq:

- The United States sent 248,000 troops.
- Britain sent 45,000.
- Australia sent 2,000.
- Spain sent 1,300.
- Denmark sent 500.
- Poland sent 194.

As many as 70,000 Kurdish militia fighters from northern Iraq also took part in the fighting.

17

The Fall of Baghdad

Iraqi president Saddam Hussein with his two sons, Uday (left) and Qusay (right). Saddam's sons were two of his most important lieutenants.

On April 9, 2003, coalition forces captured the Iraqi capital city, Baghdad. President Saddam Hussein and his sons, Uday and Qusay, who were among his most important lieutenants, had already fled. Other leaders of Saddam's regime had also left or been killed. The coalition had accomplished one of its aims: to topple Saddam from power. In the following days, Kurdish fighters and coalition forces took control of the northern cities of Kirkuk and Mosul. As a military exercise, the invasion was a success.

AIMS OF THE COALITION

The coalition had gone to war in Iraq with two main aims: to topple Saddam and to prevent him from making WMDs that could be used to attack his enemies. In fact, the allies did not completely agree on the aims of the war: Prime Minister Tony Blair

Regime change?

"The stated policy of the United States is regime change ... However, if Hussein were to meet all the conditions of the United Nations ... that in itself will signal the regime has changed."
President George W. Bush, speaking on October 21, 2002.

"So far as our objective, it is disarmament, not regime change—that is our objective. Now I happen to believe the regime of Saddam is a very brutal and repressive regime, I think it does enormous damage to the Iraqi people ... [but our purpose] is disarmament of weapons of mass destruction; it is not regime change."
British prime minister Tony Blair, January 29, 2003.

TIMELINE

INTELLIGENCE AND WMDs, 2003–2006

February 3, 2003 ▶ UK government publishes a dossier (later called the "dodgy dossier") about Iraq's WMDs.

uly 17, 2003 ▶ British prime minister Tony Blair tells the US Congress that he is sure history will prove the coalition to have acted well, even if no WMDs are found.

October 18, 2004 ▶ Prime minster Tony Blair apologizes for "intelligence errors" that led him to think that Iraq had WMDs.

April 7, 2006 ▶ President Bush admits that intelligence on WMDs was wrong and says he is as sorry as anyone for the mistake.

refused to say that regime change was one of his aims, while President Bush admitted it was something he wanted to achieve. But both leaders said the main reason for the invasion was that Iraq had been making WMDs, despite being told many times by the UN that it must stop.

After being draped in a US flag, this statue of Saddam was pulled over by an American tank. Hundreds of Iraqis immediately rushed forward to kick and beat the statue as it lay on the ground.

THE HUNT FOR WMDs

As soon as the invasion was over, the coalition began to look for evidence of Iraqi WMDs. The hunt went on for over a year. On September 30, 2004, the group that had been given the job of searching Iraq for banned weapons, the Iraq Survey Group, reported that it had "not found evidence that Saddam Hussein possessed WMD stocks in 2003." The survey group also said that any WMDs that were still undiscovered were "not of a militarily significant capability."

CROSS-REFERENCE
WMDs: PAGES 12–13
THE CAPTURE OF SADDAM: PAGES 26–27

"Mission Accomplished"

President George W. Bush speaks to crew members of the USS Abraham Lincoln. *His message is clearly seen in the background.*

On May 1, 2003, President George W. Bush landed on the deck of the aircraft carrier USS *Abraham Lincoln* in the Persian Gulf. He announced that it was "mission accomplished" for the Allied forces, and that "major combat operations" were finished. President Bush was correct to say that the military invasion was largely complete, but there were still many challenges to overcome before the invasion of Iraq could be considered a success.

CELEBRATIONS AND RESENTMENTS

Many Iraqis celebrated Saddam's downfall. The Kurds and Shia, who make up most of Iraq's population, were mostly glad he was gone. In Baghdad's Firdos Square, a determined crowd hauled down one particularly large and famous statue of Saddam. Men began to beat it with their shoes—an especially insulting gesture in Arab countries. However, very few Iraqis backed the invasion completely:

- Even if they had wanted to get rid of Saddam, many Iraqis wished that it had not taken an invasion by foreign troops to end his rule.
- Sunni Muslims had dominated the government, civil service, and armed forces under Saddam. They largely saw the invasion as a defeat.
- Some Muslim Iraqis wished that non-Muslims had not come to Iraq, which is home to some of Islam's holiest shrines.

THE SPREAD OF LAWLESSNESS

Saddam had been a cruel ruler, who regularly used violence to keep a tight grip on power. When his regime was defeated, it was not clear what would replace it. Local rulers

The Ba'ath Party

Until the coalition invasion, the Ba'ath Party and its leader, Saddam Hussein, governed Iraq. The Ba'ath Party was founded in the 1940s with the aim of linking all Arabs together. It developed branches in various countries but was strongest in Syria and Iraq. It came to power in Iraq in 1963 and again in 1968. Under Saddam, it was a mainly Sunni organization, even though most Iraqis are Shia.

in some areas began to attack one another, battling over which areas they would control. At the same time, looting became commonplace, with private property and national treasures being stolen. For example, thousands of valuable ancient artefacts were stolen from the Iraqi National Museum and are still turning up for sale around the world today.

CROSS-REFERENCE DE-BA'ATHIFICATION: PAGES 22–23

A room in the National Library in Baghdad lies in ruins after looters ransacked it looking for anything of value.

Dismantling Saddam's Regime

MAY 22, 2003

On May 22, 2003 the UN Security Council agreed to Resolution 1483. The resolution recognized that the United States and Britain were "occupying powers under unified command" and were now responsible for Iraq. In effect, the resolution recognized that the members of the coalition were the new, temporary rulers of Iraq. It also ended UN sanctions against Iraq and transferred the income from Iraq's oil sales to the Coalition Provisional Authority, which had replaced Saddam's government.

DE-BA'ATHIFICATION
The Ba'ath Party had run Iraq since 1968 and been a key part of Saddam's rule. The coalition decided it must be abolished and Ba'ath Party members removed from positions of power. Junior officials were told to leave their jobs. Coalition forces hunted down higher-ranking officials who had played an active part in Saddam's brutal regime, with the aim of punishing them for their actions.

DISBANDING THE ARMY AND POLICE
Until the invasion, the Iraqi army and police force had been used by Saddam to keep control of the country. Both had used violence against their fellow Iraqis many times, and among the soldiers and policemen were large numbers of Saddam's supporters. In 2003, the coalition decided to disband the army and police force.

With no effective police force alongside them, coalition soldiers began to struggle to keep control. Some areas of the country, for example, the Baghdad suburb of Sadr City, quickly became no-go zones—areas where coalition forces dared not go in case they were attacked. In Baghdad, almost all non-Iraqis were forced to live inside a heavily fortified area called the "Green Zone" for their own safety.

US soldiers on patrol in Baghdad in May 2003. Coalition forces were beginning to find it increasingly hard to keep order in parts of Iraq.

SADDAM'S REGIME, 1968–2003

July 17, 1968 ▶ Saddam Hussein becomes vice president of Iraq.

July 16, 1979 ▶ Saddam Hussein becomes secretary general of the Ba'ath Party and president of Iraq.

April 9, 2003 ▶ Baghdad is captured by coalition forces, ending Saddam's rule.

April 15, 2003 ▶ Saddam's hometown, Tikrit, is captured by coalition forces. Many of Saddam's most important supporters came from Tikrit, and it was among his most loyal bases.

GROWTH OF THE INSURGENCY

By 2004, the violence in Iraq had steadily become worse. There was an increase in the number of attacks both on coalition forces and on the new Iraqi government. These attacks became known as the insurgency. Insurgents were a combination of local leaders and foreign fighters. Some were Sunnis unhappy at losing control of Iraq, some were local warlords trying to gain as much territory as possible, and some came to attack the United States and its allies, who they saw as the enemies of Islam.

CROSS-REFERENCE
UN SANCTIONS: PAGES 10–11
THE BA'ATH PARTY: PAGES 20–21

An Iraqi policeman stands beside the burnt-out wreckage of a police car in 2004. The car had been set on fire during an insurgent attack the night before.

Pack of cards

In April 2003, US forces issued a list of the 55 most-wanted members of the former Iraqi regime in the form of a deck of cards. Top of the most-wanted list were Saddam Hussein, his sons, Uday and Qusay, his secretary, Abid Hamid Mahmud, and Ali Hassan al-Majid—known as "Chemical Ali" for his part in the gas attacks on the Kurds in 1988 (see page 6).

Attack on the UN Embassy

AUGUST 19, 2003

This photo was taken moments after the bomb attack on the UN building in Baghdad, on August 19, 2003.

On August 19, 2003, insurgents launched a deadly bomb attack on the UN headquarters in Baghdad. The UN base was inside the city's Green Zone, which had been considered a largely safe area. A suicide bomber drove a large truck loaded with explosives to the offices, then set off his bomb. The huge explosion ripped into three floors of the building, including the office of the UN's senior representative in Iraq, Sergio Vieira de Mello. He, and at least 16 others, were killed by the blast.

BOMBINGS

The explosive used in the UN headquarters bombing probably came from pre-invasion Iraqi army stores. Many insurgents were Saddam supporters, former members of the

army who knew how to use explosives. Throughout late 2003, bombings became increasingly common in Iraq. The insurgents targeted the coalition forces, recruiting offices for the new Iraqi police and army, and foreign diplomats. On August 7, 2003, bombers

Violence in Iraq

"Nothing can excuse this act of unprovoked and murderous violence against men and women who went to Iraq ... to help the Iraqi people."
Kofi Annan, UN secretary general, speaking on August 20, 2003, about the attack on the UN embassy.

"Many Iraqis are too afraid of kidnappings to take their children to school or to go to work."
Zaki Chehab, author of *Iraq Ablaze—Inside the Insurgency* (Tauris, 2005).

Jordanian terrorist Abu Musab al-Zarqawi was behind many of the kidnappings and murders of foreigners in Iraq.

attacked the Jordanian embassy in Baghdad. In Najaf, central Iraq, a car bomb placed near one of the holiest shrines for Shia Muslims killed 125 people, including the Shia leader Ayatollah Mohammed Baqr al-Hakim. There were hundreds of other bombings.

KIDNAPPINGS

Through 2003 and 2004, the number of violent kidnappings in Iraq increased. There were many high-profile kidnappings of non-Iraqis, often by groups allied to the Muslim terrorist organization al-Qaeda. These groups wanted all non-Muslims to leave Iraq. When their demands were not met, they beheaded their victims. The leader of many of these kidnappings was a Jordanian terrorist called Abu Musab al-Zarqawi.

Iraqis also suffered very high numbers of kidnappings—reportedly as many as 30 a day. Sometimes people were kidnapped for money. Other kidnappings were for revenge: the victims either disappeared or their bodies were later found dumped at the side of a road.

CROSS-REFERENCE DISBANDING THE ARMY AND POLICE FORCE: PAGES 22–23

The Capture of Saddam

DECEMBER 13, 2003

On December 13, 2003, in Operation Red Dawn, coalition forces captured former president Saddam Hussein. He had been on the run since April and was finally discovered hiding at the bottom of a deep hole near his hometown of Tikrit. The capture of Saddam was important: while he was still free, his supporters had been able to hope that he (and they) might somehow regain power.

SADDAM ON TRIAL

Saddam's capture meant he could be tried for actions taken when he had ruled Iraq. His most notorious acts included

- Ordering a massacre in the Shia town of Dujail after a failed assassination attempt there in 1982. In reprisal, 148 local males were killed, around 1,500 people were jailed and tortured, and other residents were sent to live in the desert. The town was destroyed, along with 390 square miles (1,000 square kilometers) of farmland.
- The al-Anfal campaign against the Kurds between 1987 and 1989 (see pages 6–7).
- Brutally crushing revolts by Kurds and Shias in 1991.

Saddam was first tried for the Dujail massacre. The trial began in October 2005 and took over a year. His defense was that he had been illegally overthrown and was still the president of Iraq so the court did not have the right to try him. Nonetheless, in November 2006 the five judges handed down their verdict: guilty. Saddam was sentenced to death by hanging and on December 30, was executed.

HUNTING DOWN THE REGIME'S LEADERS

Saddam's capture and execution were only part of the hunting down of important members of his regime. On July 22, 2003, coalition forces had killed Saddam's sons, Uday and

Saddam Hussein on trial for crimes committed when he was president of Iraq.

TIMELINE	SADDAM'S CRIMES, 1982–1991
July 8, 1982	▶ A failed assassination attempt on Saddam Hussein in Dujail is punished by a massacre in the town.
1987–1989	▶ The al-Anfal campaign against the Kurds.
1991	▶ Between 60,000 and 130,000 southern Shia and 30,000 to 60,000 Kurds are killed by Saddam's forces after rebellions against him.

Qusay. In August 2003, Saddam's cousin Ali Hassan al-Majid, a former defense minister and, briefly, governor of Kuwait—was captured. He was sentenced to death in 2007 for his part in the al-Anfal campaign. In all, over 300 leaders of Saddam's regime were killed or captured.

In Sadr City, a Shia district of Baghdad, Iraqis celebrate Saddam's death sentence. Saddam was found guilty of ordering the massacre of Shia people in the town of Dujail in 1982.

CROSS-REFERENCE
THE AL-ANFAL CAMPAIGN, KURDISH AND SHIA REBELLIONS:
PAGES 6–7

Sunni violence

The capture and trial of leaders of Saddam's regime created anger among some Sunni groups and contributed to the increase in violence. For example:

- In February 2004, more than 100 people were killed in Irbil by Sunni suicide attacks on the offices of the main Kurdish parties.
- In March 2004, Sunni suicide bombers attacked people celebrating a Shia festival in Karbala and Baghdad, killing 170 people.

Abu Ghraib

On March 21, 2004, coalition commanders in Iraq announced that six of their soldiers who worked at the Abu Ghraib prison in Baghdad had been charged with mistreating prisoners. Then, in late April, photos began to emerge of hooded prisoners being abused and tortured by smiling military police officers. Suddenly, Abu Ghraib prison was headline news.

ABUSE AND TORTURE

The photos showed Iraqi prisoners, many of them naked apart from hoods over their heads. They were being sat on, punched, forced to stand on wooden blocks with their arms out straight, showered with cold water, and mistreated in other ways. Reports suggested that there had also been far worse abuses. Many guards in the photos appeared to be enjoying what they were doing. They were smiling— one man was even shown grinning and giving a thumbs-up over the corpse of a prisoner who had died.

THE AUTHORITIES REACT

The coalition authorities acted quickly to arrest and try those responsible for the abuse and torture of the prisoners. In total, 10 soldiers were later found

Horrified Iraqis examine newspaper photos showing the abuse and torture of prisoners at Abu Ghraib prison.

guilty and sentenced to prison terms ranging from 90 days to 10 years. Other guards and officers were fined and demoted as a result of the investigation.

EFFECTS OF THE ABU GHRAIB ABUSE

The prisoner abuse at Abu Ghraib had a terrible effect on the coalition's reputation, both in Iraq and around the world. Iraqis, and people everywhere, were horrified. The coalition had partly justified its invasion of Iraq by telling people how terrible things were under Saddam—who had tortured and killed those who would not support him. Now coalition soldiers appeared to be behaving in a similar way. Abu Ghraib caused an increase in anger and resentment at the coalition forces inside Iraq.

Private Lynddie England is led away after being found guilty of abusing prisoners at Abu Ghraib prison.

CROSS-REFERENCE
JUSTIFICATIONS
FOR WAR: PAGES
18–19

Scandal at Abu Ghraib

"They said we will make you wish to die and it will not happen ... They ordered me to thank Jesus that I'm alive ... I said to him, 'I believe in Allah.' So he said, 'But I believe in torture and I will torture you.'"
Iraqi prisoner Ameen Saeed Al-Sheikh describes his experiences in Abu Ghraib.

"So what would I tell the people of Iraq? This [was] wrong. This [was] reprehensible. But this is not representative of the 150,000 soldiers that are over here."
General Mark Kimmitt, interviewed on US television.

"To those Iraqis who were mistreated by members of US armed forces, I offer my deepest apology. It was un-American. And it was inconsistent with the values of our nation."
US Secretary of Defense Donald Rumsfeld, May 7, 2004.

Transfer of Power

JUNE 28, 2004

On June 28, 2004, the Coalition Provisional Authority (CPA) handed power to an interim Iraqi government. This meant that Iraqis once again had some control over their own country. The interim government contained members of the Shia, Sunni, and Kurd communities. The new prime minister was a Shia, Iyad Allawi. The deputy prime minister was a Kurd, Barham Salih. The new president was a Sunni, Ghazi Mashal Ajil al-Yawer.

THE INTERIM GOVERNMENT

The interim government was to govern Iraq until a vote could be held to choose members of an elected government. Iraq did not have a constitution, so the interim government worked under a set of rules put together by a committee of Iraqis. The most important of these rules were
- All Iraqis were equal before the law.
- Freedom of speech was guaranteed.
- Iraq was to have a free press and media, but individuals also had the right to privacy.
- Everyone accused of a crime had the right to a fair, open trial.
- Unlawful arrest, detention, cruel punishment, and torture were all illegal.
- Arabic and Kurdish were to be Iraq's official languages.

Iraq's interim prime minister, Iyad Allawi, speaks to the press in December 2004.

CALLS FOR ELECTIONS

Soon after the interim government took power, calls began to grow for elections to be held. Many people wanted an elected Iraqi government to be formed. Although this was scheduled to happen by January 2005, many Iraqis were impatient for the chance to vote in an election and thought that the interim government should move more quickly.

Targeting the police

In 2004, the Iraqi police force was made up almost entirely of new recruits, who were regularly attacked by insurgents. The insurgents did not want Iraqis to work with coalition forces, who they thought should leave Iraq immediately. Many police recruiting offices were hit by bomb attacks, and hundreds of those who had wanted to join up were killed.

VIOLENCE

The biggest challenge facing the interim government was the worsening violence inside Iraq. Large areas of the country were still under the control of local leaders, some of whom were insurgents. Two particular trouble spots were the Shia holy city of Najaf and the Sunni stronghold of Fallujah. In Najaf, the Mehdi Army had been formed by the Shia leader Muqtada al-Sadr to support Shia interests. The Mehdi Army fought several battles against coalition troops in April, May, and August of 2004. In Fallujah, Sunni insurgents had largely taken control of the city by the middle of 2004.

CROSS-REFERENCE
THE BATTLE FOR FALLUJAH: PAGES 32–33
ELECTIONS: PAGES 34–35

An armored vehicle on patrol in the streets of Najaf, where there were violent clashes between coalition forces and Shia militias during 2004.

The Battle for Fallujah

On November 8, 2004, coalition forces launched Operation Phantom Fury—a major attack on the Sunni city of Fallujah. It was the start of what would become known as the Second Battle of Fallujah. The First Battle of Fallujah had ended in April 2004, when coalition troops had left the city in the hands of local Iraqi forces.

REASONS FOR THE ATTACK

Fallujah was a Sunni stronghold. As Sunni resentment of the coalition grew, Fallujah attracted increasing numbers of insurgents—both Iraqis and foreign fighters. Among them was Abu Musab al-Zarqawi, who led al-Qaeda in Iraq. Through the middle of 2004, the insurgents built up their forces, and by late September, there were estimated to be thousands of foreign fighters in Fallujah. They had turned the city into a fortress. The coalition realized it needed to retake control of Fallujah if it was to have any hope of defeating the insurgents in Iraq.

FOREIGN FIGHTERS

Muslim fighters had been drawn to Fallujah by the opportunity to attack coalition forces. They saw the United States, whose soldiers made up most of the coalition army, as their enemy. They considered the United States to be anti-Arab and anti-Muslim because it supported the Jewish country Israel in conflicts with its Muslim Arab neighbors. Many of the foreign fighters were also angry that non-Muslims were occupying a land that contained Muslim holy sites.

CAPTURING FALLUJAH

The battle for Fallujah lasted from November 8 to December 23. It was one of the bloodiest battles of the entire Iraq War. Most of the civilians

NOVEMBER 8, 2004

Doorway by doorway, street by street, coalition soldiers fight their way into the Sunni city of Fallujah in November 2004.

in the city, and some of the insurgent leaders, fled before the battle began. The coalition set up checkpoints around the city to stop insurgents from escaping, then its forces fought their way through Fallujah's streets. By November 16, most of the fighting was over. The battle ended with coalition forces taking control of the city, and many al-Qaeda fighters being killed. Al-Zarqawi, however, escaped.

This woman has fled from the battle in Fallujah and has arrived in a temporary refugee camp set up for the city's people. The plastic bags contain all her belongings.

CROSS-REFERENCE VIOLENCE DURING THE TRANSFER OF POWER: PAGES 30–31

Life in Fallujah

Today, opinions are divided about what life is like in Fallujah, which still is under tight security controls:

"The evidence points to Fallujah [now] being a model for other cities in terms of security and stability."
Sa'ad Awad, mayor of Fallujah, December 20, 2007.

"The Americans provide us with nothing. They bring us only destruction."
A mother in a Fallujah hospital, 2008.

Elections

Iraqis line up by the hundreds to cast votes in the January 2005 elections. Turnout ranged from 89 percent in the Kurdish region of Dahuk to 2 percent in the Sunni region of Anbar. Overall, very few Sunnis voted.

In January 2005, the first free elections for 50 years were held in Iraq. Many observers feared they would be ruined by violence, but in the end the elections were mostly peaceful.

The vote was to elect members of a Transitional National Assembly. The assembly's job would be to agree on a new constitution for Iraq and then to organize further elections.

ELECTION RESULTS

The election results were split largely along ethnic and religious lines. Most of the seats in the assembly were divided between Shia and Kurdish parties. The largest Shia group got 48 percent of the vote and 140 of 275 seats, with a second Shia group getting an additional 40 seats. The Kurdish Alliance got 28 percent of the vote and 75 seats. Almost all Sunnis boycotted the elections, feeling that they did not want to take part in a contest that the Shia and Kurds would inevitably win. The Sunni group ended up with just five seats.

VIOLENCE CONTINUES

Despite the elections, the violence in Iraq continued and even began to get worse. The violence was increasingly the result of conflict between Iraq's different religions and tribes. In an effort to stem the violence by showing that Iraqis from different groups could work together, the assembly chose the Kurdish leader Jalal Talabani (who was also a Sunni) as president. Ibrahim Jaafari, a Shia, was named as prime minister.

A NEW CONSTITUTION

Iraqis approved their new constitution in a referendum in October 2005. Iraq was to be organized into 18 provinces, some of which could one day join together to become regions. The Shia and Kurds overwhelmingly supported the constitution. The Sunnis rejected it because they felt the new constitution would not give them enough power. However, the Sunnis were outvoted, and the new constitution was adopted.

POST-ELECTION VIOLENCE, 2005

February 28, 2005 ▶ 125 people are killed by a massive car bomb in Al-Hilla, central Iraq—the worst incident since the invasion.

May 2005 ▶ There is a surge in car bombings, bomb explosions, and shootings; Iraqi ministries put the civilian death toll for May at 672, up from 364 in April.

July 2005 ▶ A study by the non-governmental Iraq Body Count organization estimates that nearly 25,000 Iraqi civilians have been killed since the 2003 invasion. (These figures are widely disputed.)

August 2005 ▶ More than 1,000 people are killed during a stampede at a Shia ceremony in Baghdad.

September 2005 ▶ 182 people are killed in attacks in Baghdad, including a car bomb attack on a group of workers in a mainly Shia district.

Referendum on the new Iraqi constitution

Overall, 78 percent of voters backed Iraq's new constitution and 21 percent rejected it, with a 63 percent turnout.
- **15 of 18 provinces voted "Yes".**
- **There were "No" vote majorities in three Sunni provinces: a 96 percent rejection in Anbar, 81 percent in Salahuddin, and 55 percent in Nineveh.**

MORE ELECTIONS

Fresh elections were held on December 15, 2005. Jalal Talabani was elected president. By January 20, 2006 all the votes had been counted and checked, and the Shia-led United Iraqi Alliance emerged as the winner. Because the Alliance had won less than half the votes, it could not form a government alone. After four months of negotiations over who would work with whom, on April 22, 2006, Shia leader Nouri al-Maliki formed a new government.

Jalal Talabani (left) is congratulated by Ibrahim Jaafari after being chosen by the Transitional National Assembly to be president of Iraq.

CROSS-REFERENCE
TRANSFER OF POWER AND CALLS FOR ELECTIONS: PAGES 30–31

Attack on the al-Askari Mosque

At 6.55 a.m. on February 22, 2006, there was an explosion at the al-Askari mosque, in the Iraqi city of Samarra. The blast destroyed the mosque's famous golden dome and badly damaged three-quarters of the rest of the building. The explosion was the result of a bomb planted at the mosque by militants. The militants had entered the building the previous night, tied up the guards, and set the explosives before fleeing.

A Shia holy site

The militants had targeted the al-Askari mosque because it is one of Shia Islam's holiest sites. It houses the shrines of the tenth and eleventh imams, or leaders, of the Shia Muslims. Nearby is a second mosque, associated with the twelfth imam. Although it is a Shia holy site, the mosque is in the city of Samarra, which is mainly Sunni.

Aims of the bombers

The bombing of the mosque was the work of an al-Qaeda cell in Iraq. The militants hoped that they would stir up violence between the Shia and Sunni communities. Their aim was to make the situation in Iraq so violent and unmanageable that the coalition would withdraw its forces. They hoped this would leave them free to make Iraq a country run according to extreme Islamic laws.

Aftermath of the bombing

The bombing led to a huge increase in violence. Within a day, in Baghdad alone 19 Sunni mosques had been attacked, one cleric murdered, and

The golden dome of the al-Askari mosque, flanked by two golden minarets (towers), in the days before it was destroyed by bombers.

Militant success?

"They will fail to draw the Iraqi people into civil war, as they have failed in the past." Muwafaq al-Rubaie, an Iraqi national security adviser, speaks about the militants who were behind the attack on the al-Askari mosque, February 22, 2006.

another kidnapped. The violence became so bad that on February 23, President Talabani warned that the country was on the edge of civil war. People in mixed areas, where Sunni and Shia lived side by side, began leaving because they feared being attacked by their neighbors. The government started to impose curfews—first at night, then during the day as well—keeping people indoors, where they could not take part in violent attacks. Even so, by February 27, over 300 people had been killed and over 400 injured in violent attacks, and hundreds of mosques had been blown up.

The ruined dome of the al-Askari mosque after the February 2006 bombing.

CROSS-REFERENCE AL-QAEDA IN IRAQ: PAGES 24–25, 32–33

THE SITUATION CALMS

Iraq's Shia leaders appealed for calm and restraint. This, and the government curfews, gradually led to a decrease in the violence. Bombings and attacks between Sunni and Shia continued, but Iraq stepped back from the brink of civil war.

Troop Surge

During a television speech to the American people on January 10, 2007, President Bush announced what later became known as a "troop surge" in Iraq—a big increase in the number of US soldiers in the coalition. The president said that he was sending an additional 20,000 soldiers. Their aim was to work with the Iraqi security forces to bring an end to the violence that had dogged Baghdad and the surrounding area since 2003.

REASONS FOR THE TROOP SURGE

The troop surge was needed because it seemed that the coalition's invasion of Iraq might end in failure. The violence after the bombing of the al-Askari mosque in 2006 had died down but continued to simmer. Many Iraqis still did not have electricity, gas, or running water in their homes, and many lived in worse conditions than had existed before the invasion. Fear of violence made normal life impossible, with people scared to be on the streets, especially after dark.

US ELECTIONS

On November 7, 2006, there were midterm elections in the United States. The results were a disaster for President Bush's Republican Party. The rival Democratic Party gained control of both houses of the legislature, the Senate and the House of Representatives. Most commentators agreed that one of the main reasons for the Republican defeat was that Americans were unhappy about the war in Iraq. The president knew he had to act if the Republicans were to have a chance in the next elections.

JANUARY 10, 2007

A coalition soldier hands out Iraqi flags to children in 2007, attempting to show that coalition forces and Iraqis can be friendly to one another.

TIMELINE	TROOP SURGE, 2006–2008
November 7, 2006	▶ The US midterm elections end in poor results for the Republicans.
December 6, 2006	▶ The Iraq Study Group presents a report suggesting that an increase in troop numbers is needed.
January 10, 2007	▶ President Bush announces a troop surge.
January–May 2007	▶ Five extra divisions of US troops (20,000 soldiers) arrive in Iraq.
September 10, 2007	▶ US general David Petraeus reports that the surge is meeting its objectives.
February 16, 2008	▶ Iraq's defense minister tells reporters the surge is "working very well".

EFFECTS OF THE TROOP SURGE

In the short term, the surge did not seem to have a big effect. Three months after it started, Iraqi security forces and coalition troops still controlled less than a third of Baghdad. Later in 2007 and into 2008, though, the surge began to bear fruit. The security situation improved, with less violence in many areas. As the streets became safer, it became easier to bring back basic services such as water and electricity, at least in the cities. For some Iraqis, life began to return to normal.

Christmas decorations on sale in a Baghdad market in December 2007. Markets such as this one had been in danger from bombers, but by the end of 2007, security in Baghdad had begun to improve.

CROSS-REFERENCE
VIOLENCE AFTER THE ATTACK ON THE AL-ASKARI MOSQUE: PAGES 36–37

Safer Baghdad

"With Iraqis in the lead, our forces will help secure [Baghdad] by chasing down the terrorists, insurgents, and the roaming death squads."
President George W. Bush, January 23, 2007.

A Divided Government

On August 1, 2007 the main Sunni political group in Iraq withdrew from the government. Prime Minister Nouri al-Maliki lost six Sunni ministers. Earlier in the year, in April, five ministers who were followers of Shia leader Muqtada al-Sadr had already resigned. Prime Minster Maliki's government seemed to be losing support from all sides of the Iraqi parliament. The government began to look increasingly unstable.

REASONS FOR THE RESIGNATIONS

The Sunnis had threatened to quit a week earlier unless the government agreed to a list of 12 demands. The most important of these were

- Releasing Sunni prisoners held without charge in US and Iraqi detention centers.
- Dissolving and disarming all militias, as well as any army officers or enlisted military personnel linked to militias. (Since many militias were Shia, this would have benefited the Sunnis.)
- Appointing experienced, qualified Iraqis to work in government jobs (since the government had been run mainly by Sunnis until 2003, it was mainly Sunnis who were experienced and qualified).
- Improving relations with other Arab states (in which Sunnis were the majority).

When the prime minister did not agree, the Sunnis resigned.

FINDING A WAY FORWARD

Iraq's parliament tried to find a way to bring Sunni politicians back into the government. In January 2008, it passed legislation allowing former officials from Saddam Hussein's Ba'ath Party to be given government jobs. Almost all Ba'athist officials were Sunni. Partly as a result, in July 2008 the Iraqi Accordance Front rejoined the government, almost a year after it had pulled out.

There was further encouragement for the Sunnis later in the year. Some of the Sunni militias, called

Shia leader Muqtada al-Sadr speaks to his supporters during Friday prayers. In April 2007, five of his supporters resigned from the Iraqi government.

CROSS-REFERENCE
THE ELECTIONS:
PAGES 34–35

TIMELINE	IRAQ'S ELECTED GOVERNMENT, 2006–2008

April 22, 2006 ▶ Iraq's first elected government for 40 years takes power. It includes Shia, Sunni, and Kurdish ministers.

April 2007 ▶ Five Sadrist (Shia) ministers resign.

April 2007 ▶ Six Sunni ministers resign.

September 13, 2007 ▶ Sheikh Abdul Sattar is assassinated by a roadside bomb. The sheikh had led the fight against al-Qaeda and encouraged Sunnis to join the Iraqi police force, making him a target for insurgents.

July 2008 ▶ Sunni politicians rejoin the government.

Improved security

In a sign of Iraq's improved security during 2008, in September, coalition forces handed over control of the western province of Anbar to the Iraqi government. Once a flashpoint of the insurgency, then an al-Qaeda stronghold, Anbar was the first Sunni province to be returned to government control.

Awakening Councils, had joined in the fight against al-Qaeda. In October, members of the Baghdad Awakening Council, estimated to number about 54,000, became government employees. The members of other Awakening Council militia groups seemed set to follow.

A delegation of sheikhs (elders) from Anbar province in Iraq leave the White House in Washington, DC, after a meeting with President George W. Bush in 2008 about local elections and uprisings.

Iran's President Visits Iraq

MARCH 2, 2008

On March 2, 2008, the president of neighboring Iran, Mahmoud Ahmadinejad, paid a visit to Iraq. No Iranian leader had visited Iraq since Iran had become an Islamic republic in 1979. The two countries had fought a long, bitter, and painful war (started by the Iraqi leader Saddam Hussein) between 1980 and 1988. Iran had also been accused of stirring up trouble inside Iraq since the invasion by supporting Shia militants. President Ahmadinejad's visit stirred up bitter feelings among those who did not want closer links between Iran and Iraq.

HEREDITARY RULERS

Among those who feared closer links between the two countries were the hereditary rulers of other Middle Eastern countries. In 1979, Iranians had overthrown their own hereditary ruler, the shah, and had turned Iran into an Islamic republic—a country run according to Islamic rules. This made the hereditary leaders of other countries in the Middle East nervous. What if their people decided that this was a good idea? When Saddam attacked Iran in 1980, they decided to support him, loaning him vast sums of money so that he could buy weapons for the war.

President Ahmadinejad's visit showed that Iran, a country that holds regular elections to help choose its political

President Ahmadinejad of Iran (left) talks to Iraqi president Talabani during his visit to Iraq in 2008.

leaders, was developing links with democratic Iraq. The number of Middle Eastern countries where people could vote for their leaders was growing.

THE SUNNI WORLD

The conflict between Iran and Iraq had been partly religious. Saddam and his supporters, and most other countries in the Muslim world, were Sunnis. Almost all Iranians, and most Iraqis, are Shia Muslims. Iraq had been the Sunni world's front line in

Brotherly talks

"We had very good talks that were friendly and brotherly. We have mutual understandings and views in all fields, and both sides plan to improve relations as much as possible."
Iranian president Mahmoud Ahmadinejad during his visit to Iraq, March 2–3, 2008.

TIMELINE

IRAN–IRAQ RELATIONS, 1975–2008

March 6, 1975 ▶ Iran and Iraq sign the Algiers Accord to settle a dispute over the border between the two countries.

1980–1988 ▶ War between Iran and Iraq claims between 500,000 and a million lives.

2003 ▶ Saddam Hussein is overthrown.

November 21, 2005 ▶ Iraqi president Talabani visits Iran for talks.

March 2, 2008 ▶ Iranian president Ahmadinejad visits Iraq.

its conflict with the Shia. Now, Iraq too was run by a Shia government; the front line in the religious conflict seemed to be rolling back. Iraq's Sunnis, who until 2003 had been in charge, now found themselves outnumbered and surrounded by Shia.

THE KURDS

The Kurds had established their own region, Kurdistan, in northern Iraq. But many Kurds hoped that one day they would have their own country. This would include not only northern Iraq, but also the other places where the 15 to 20 million Kurds live: in Armenia, Turkey, Syria—and Iran. The Shia-led governments of Iraq and Iran would not want to lose their Kurdish territory, and closer links between them were likely to make it harder for the Kurds to achieve their aims.

CROSS-REFERENCE
THE WAR WITH IRAN: PAGES 4–5
THE KURDS: PAGES 6–7

Kurds in northern Iraq celebrate the Kurdish new year, Newroz, on March 20, 2009. They are carrying torches in a procession up a mountain, which is draped in the flag of Iraqi Kurdistan. Newroz is also celebrated in Turkey, Iran, and other countries where Kurds live.

Planned Withdrawal

Iraqi policemen at their graduation ceremony in the northern city of Mosul. As Iraq's police force grew and security improved, it became possible to plan the withdrawal of coalition forces

On November 27, 2008, the Iraqi parliament agreed to a date for all coalition forces to leave Iraq: December 31, 2011. Part of the reason was Iraq's improved security situation. Although killings, bombings, and kidnappings continued, the Iraqi police and army were increasingly able to keep order without the coalition's help. Basic services such as water and power became more commonly available, and people felt safer being on the streets.

STRIKING THE DEAL

At first, not all Iraqis had supported the planned withdrawal:

- Sunnis had worried that without coalition protection, they would be at the mercy of the Shia and Kurds. In the end, the Sunnis were given guarantees of their safety.
- Some Shia said that the coalition should leave Iraq immediately. Most were won over by the fact that under the deal, coalition forces had to leave Iraqi cities, towns, and

Governing Iraq

What type of government do most Iraqis want? This 2009 poll gives some idea of how the country's three main groups see things. The results of a 2007 poll asking the same question are in parentheses.

	Kurds %	Shia %	Sunni %
One strong leader for life	12 (25)	9 (19)	20 (58)
Islamic state run to religious rules	15 (10)	26 (40)	11 (4)
Democracy in which leader can be replaced	71 (65)	62 (41)	65 (38)
No answer	2	3	4

TIMELINE

COALITION DEPARTURE, 2008–2009

July 2008 ▶ Prime Minister Maliki suggests setting a timetable for the withdrawal of coalition troops.

ember 2008 ▶ The Iraqi parliament decides that all coalition troops will leave the country by the end of 2011.

anuary 2009 ▶ Iraq takes control of security in Baghdad's Green Zone and assumes more powers over foreign troops based in the country.

bruary 2009 ▶ Prime Minister Maliki's supporters score big wins in provincial elections, which pass with little violence.

March 2009 ▶ President Barack Obama announces the withdrawal of most US troops by August 31, 2010. Up to 50,000 will stay to advise Iraqi forces and protect US interests, leaving by the end of 2011.

villages by June 30, 2009. Only the Shia led by Muqtada al-Sadr—known as the Sadrists—continued to reject the deal. The Sadrists were closely linked with Iran. Prime Minister Maliki's friendly relationship with Iran meant he could face down the Sadrist politicians.

IMPROVEMENTS IN IRAQI LIFE

By 2009, life had improved for many Iraqis. A poll in February showed that many of them were starting to feel confident about a better future. For example, 65 percent of Iraqis thought life was quite good or very good, compared to 39 percent in February 2007, when the violence was peaking, and 70 percent in 2004, shortly after the invasion. Despite the recent improvements, though, the number of Iraqis who thought the coalition had been right to invade Iraq had fallen, from 49 percent in 2004 to 42 percent in 2009.

CROSS-REFERENCE
IRAQ'S GOVERNMENT:
PAGES **40–41**

President Barack Obama speaks to American troops during a visit to Iraq in April 2009. President Obama aimed to bring US troops home from Iraq by 2011.

Key Figures in the Iraq War

ALI HASSAN AL-MAJID (1941–), IRAQI MINISTER

Known as "Chemical Ali" for his use of poisonous gas against Iraq's Kurds in 1988, al-Majid was Saddam's older cousin. Briefly the governor of Kuwait after the Iraqi invasion, he became Minister of the Interior in 1990, in charge of crushing post-defeat revolts, then defense minister from 1991 to 1995. On June 24, 2007, al-Majid was sentenced to death for his crimes against the Iraqi people.

NOURI AL-MALIKI (1950–), PRIME MINISTER OF IRAQ

A Shia dissident under Saddam's regime, al-Maliki was forced to flee the country in 1979 because the government planned to kill him. He returned after the coalition invasion to become a senior official of the Dawa Party, working in the interim government's de-Ba'athification program. Maliki became prime minister of Iraq on April 22, 2006.

KOFI ANNAN (1938–), UN SECRETARY-GENERAL

From 1997 to 2007, Ghana's Kofi Annan was secretary-general of the United Nations. From his first year in office, Annan was involved in trying to get Iraq to comply with the UN Security Council resolutions. Until the coalition invasion, he took an active role in negotiations for UN weapons inspection teams to enter Iraq.

TONY BLAIR (1953–), PRIME MINISTER OF THE UK

Prime minister of the United Kingdom from 1997 to 2007, Tony Blair was President George W. Bush's closest ally before and during the Iraq War. His support for the war was based on Iraq's development of WMDs and was the subject of significant opposition in Britain. When WMDs were found not to exist, his authority suffered, which led in part to his resignation.

L. PAUL BREMER (1941–), LEADER OF THE CPA

L. Paul Bremer was the US diplomat in charge of the Coalition Provisional Authority from June 2003 to June 2004. Bremer ordered the disbanding of the Iraqi army and the removal of all Ba'ath Party members from government offices, actions that many people think contributed to the violence that erupted in Iraq. Critics have also suggested that billions of dollars went unaccounted for during Bremer's term of office.

GEORGE W. BUSH (1946–), PRESIDENT OF THE UNITED STATES

Bush was the 41st US president, from 2001 to 2009, and son of the 39th president, George H. W. Bush. He was in power when al-Qaeda terrorists attacked the World Trade Center and the Pentagon in 2001 and soon afterward announced the so-called "war on terror." Bush's popularity declined dramatically during his second term, in line with the American public's perception of how the war in Iraq was going, and he left office in 2009 as one of the least popular presidents ever.

JACQUES CHIRAC (1932–), PRESIDENT OF FRANCE

Chirac, president of France between 1995 and 2007, was one of the leading opponents of the invasion of Iraq. He felt that the UN weapons inspectors needed to be given more time to find out whether Iraq still had any WMDs. Chirac thought that continued UN pressure, weapons inspections, and sanctions would eventually force Saddam to comply with UN wishes.

SADDAM HUSSEIN (1937–2006), PRESIDENT OF IRAQ

Saddam rose to fame as the right-hand man of Iraqi president Hassan al-Bakr (1968–1979). Known for his ruthlessness, he is said to have personally executed many of his rivals and enemies. In 1979, Saddam became president when Bakr resigned, and he ruled Iraq in brutal fashion from then until the coalition invasion in 2003. Captured by coalition forces in December 2003, Saddam was jailed, then put on trial for his crimes against the Iraqi people. He was found guilty and executed in December 2006.

BARACK OBAMA (1961–), PRESIDENT OF THE UNITED STATES

As a member of the Illinois Senate, Obama opposed the invasion of Iraq before it happened, attending an anti-war rally in Chicago in March 2003. During his presidential campaign, Obama said that he planned to withdraw US troops from Iraq as soon as possible; after coming to power in 2009, his administration agreed on a date for the departure of US forces.

DONALD RUMSFELD (1932–), US SECRETARY OF DEFENSE

As secretary of defense from 2001 to 2006, Rumsfeld was one of the architects of the invasion of Iraq. He wanted the invasion to be made by as small a force as possible, a decision that was later criticized because it contributed to the post-invasion violence. Rumsfeld was a controversial figure and left office in December 2006, to be replaced by Robert Gates.

JALAL TALABANI (1933–), PRESIDENT OF IRAQ

A veteran of the Kurdish battle for independence, Talabani was one of the founders of the Patriotic Union of Kurdistan. He fought in the 1961 Kurdish revolution against the Iraqi government and again in 1974–1975. He also helped to organize the Kurdish role in the coalition invasion of Iraq. In 2005, the Iraqi National Assembly appointed Talabani president of Iraq, and a year later he was elected president by the Iraqi people.

Glossary

air support   aircraft used to provide support for troops on the ground

al-Qaeda   terrorist group founded by Osama bin Laden to promote the Wahhabi (Saudi) brand of Islamic fundamentalism

Arab   group of people with Arabic as a common language, who live mainly in the Middle East and North Africa

Ba'ath Party   political party founded in the 1940s, aiming to represent the interests of all Arabs

boycott   refuse to trade or work with

cell   small unit, for example, a small group of terrorists

Central Intelligence Agency (CIA)   secret US government organization that is concerned with US relations abroad

cleric   religious leader or preacher

coalition   alliance of several groups or countries that all share the same aim

constitution   written set of laws and principles that say how a country is to be governed

curfew   time when people have to stay indoors

envoy   messenger or representative

ethnic group   a group of people united by language, customs, and tradition

Fedayeen   Arab guerrilla, especially one who fights against Israel or its allies

genocide   murder of a large group of people based on their religion or culture

hereditary   passed down through a family

insurgent   rebel

interim   in between or temporary

Kurds   people who live in a region of the Middle East spread between Turkey, Iran, Iraq, and Syria

legislature   part of a government that makes laws

Mehdi Army   paramilitary group of Shia Muslims, who support the Iraqi Shia leader Muqtada al-Sadr

Middle East   area including northeast Africa, the Arabian Peninsula, and southwest Asia, where Arabic is the most common language

militant   someone prepared to take extreme action, such as violence, to advance a cause

militia   armed force made up of civilians

munitions   supplies of weapons or ammunition

paramilitary   describes a civilian fighting force run as though it was a military organization

referendum   vote on a single issue

sanctions   trade restrictions that harm a country's people or trade, aiming to force it to change the way it acts

Senate   upper house of the US legislature, containing two senators from each state

Shia   the smaller of the two main branches of Islam. Shia Muslims regard Ali, the fourth caliph, as Muhammad's first true successor. Iran is a Shia state.

Soviet Union   powerful country with Russia at its heart, which existed from 1922 to 1991

Sunni   the biggest branch of Islam (90 percent of all Muslims)

tribe   group of people from the same place and ethnic background, who are often relatives by birth or by marriage

turnout   percentage of people who vote in an election

UN Security Council   part of the United Nations concerned with the world's security. There are five permanent members; another 10 serve two-year terms.

uranium   element needed to make nuclear weapons

weapons of mass destruction (WMDs)   weapons that can kill large numbers of people, including nuclear bombs, and chemical and biological weapons

Further Information

BOOKS

FOR CHILDREN

Barker, Geoff. *Changing World: Iraq*. Arcturus, 2008.

Downing, David. *Witness to History: The War in Iraq*. Heinemann Library, 2004.

King, John. *Iraq: Then and Now*. Raintree, 2005.

Malhotra, Sonali. *Welcome to Iraq*. Gareth Stevens, 2004.

Steele, Philip. *The Middle East*. Kingfisher, 2006.

FOR OLDER READERS AND TEACHERS

Allawi, Ali A. *The Occupation of Iraq: Winning the War, Losing the Peace*. Yale University Press, 2007.

Carlisle, Rodney P. *America at War: Iraq War*. Facts on File, 2007.

Ellis, Deborah. *Children of War: Voices of Iraqi Refugees*. Groundwood Books, 2009.

Gruber, Beth. *Ancient Iraq: Archaeology Unlocks the Secrets of Iraq's Past*. National Geographic Society, 2007.

Hashim, Ahmed. *Insurgency and Counter-Insurgency in Iraq*. C Hurst & Co, 2006.

WEBSITES

http://news.bbc.co.uk/1/hi/world/middle_east/country_profiles/791014.stm BBC country profile of Iraq

http://news.bbc.co.uk/1/hi/in_depth/middle_east/2002/conflict_with_iraq/default.stm Features and articles about Iraq

http://www.bbc.co.uk/history/recent/iraq/ The war in context

http://news.bbc.co.uk/1/shared/bsp/hi/pdfs/13_03_09_iraqpollfeb2009.pdf The results of opinion polls of Iraqis 2004–2009

http://www.krg.org The Kurdistan Regional Government site

http://www.bbc.co.uk/religion/religions/islam/subdivisions/sunnishia_1.shtml Page on the BBC website that explains the differences between Sunni and Shia Muslims

Index

Numbers in **bold** refer to photographs.